PALM BEACH COUNTY
LIBRARY SYSTEM
3650 Summit Boulevard
West Palm Beach, FL 33406-4198

21st
Century
Skills Library

REAL WORLD SCIENCE

MATTER

Heather Miller

Cherry Lake Publishing
Ann Arbor, Michigan

Published in the United States of America by Cherry Lake Publishing
Ann Arbor, Michigan
www.cherrylakepublishing.com

Content Adviser: Laura Graceffa, middle school science teacher, BA degree in science,
Vassar College; MA degrees in science and education, Brown University

Photo Credits: Cover and page 1, Charles D. Winters/Photo Researchers, Inc.; page 4,
© Dr_Flash/Shutterstock; page 6, © Ttphoto/Shutterstock; page 7, © Lori Carpenter/
Shutterstock; page 10, Adrienne Hart-Davis/Photo Researchers, Inc.; page 11,
© Geneana Bechea/Shutterstock; page 12, © Margit/Shutterstock; page 16, John Shaw/
Photo Researchers, Inc.; page 18, Perennou Nuridsany/Photo Researchers, Inc.; page 20,
© Aida Ricciardiello/Shutterstock; page 22, © Joe Gough/Shutterstock; page 24,
© stavklem/Shutterstock; page 27, Charles D. Winters / Photo Researchers, Inc.

Library of Congress Cataloging-in-Publication Data

Miller, Heather.
Matter / Heather Miller.
  p. cm.—(Real world science)
ISBN-13: 978-1-60279-460-3
ISBN-10: 1-60279-460-X
1. Matter—Juvenile literature. 2. Matter—Properties—Juvenile
literature. 3. Matter—Constitution—Juvenile literature. I. Title. II.
Series.

QC173.36.M56 2009
530.4–dc22   2008040804

*Cherry Lake Publishing would like to acknowledge the work of
The Partnership for 21st Century Skills.
Please visit* www.21stcenturyskills.org *for more information.*

TABLE OF CONTENTS

CHAPTER ONE

Solid and Sturdy

Every piece of matter, including the earth, takes up space.

Matter is anything that takes up space and has mass. The earth is

matter, and so are all the plants and animals on it. Everything in the

room you are in right now is matter. Each piece of matter takes up its own space. Two pieces of matter can never be in the same place at the same time. You can place a book on top of a chair. You can place a book under a chair. The book and the chair will always fill two separate spaces. And, the book and the chair will always be two different pieces of matter.

All matter is made up of very tiny particles called **atoms**. Atoms are so small we can't see them with a microscope. Atoms are connected to each other by **chemical bonds**. Atoms bond to form **molecules**. Molecules bond to form the matter you can see, touch, smell, and taste. There are too many molecules to count in the matter you see around you. There are more than a billion molecules in your chair, for example. Imagine how many molecules are in a skyscraper!

Rock is solid matter and water is liquid matter.

Matter exists in three main states. Matter can be solid, like a rock.

Matter can be liquid, like water. Matter can also be a gas, such as

oxygen in the air we breathe. Under the right conditions, all matter can

change state.

Solid matter is made up of molecules with tight bonds. Tight bonds

hold the molecules packed together in fixed positions. This gives the molecules very little room to move. Most of the objects you can see are solid. Your television and this book are examples of solid objects.

Solid matter keeps its shape if it is left alone. But it is possible for solid matter to change its shape, or state. A large outside force can do that. This could be something like heat or **pressure**. A beanbag chair

A beanbag chair is solid matter. It changes shape when someone sits in it.

on the floor has a certain shape. That shape can change, but only if someone sits on it or moves it into a new shape.

Many solid objects are made up of atoms with bonds that can be stretched. Stretchy chemical bonds are like tiny springs. Some fabrics are stretchy. When a stretchy fabric rests on a table, the atoms are also at rest. When the fabric is pulled, the chemical bonds are stretched. The springy bonds allow the fabric to stretch. When the fabric is released, the bonds snap back. The fabric returns to

REAL WORLD SCIENCE CHALLENGE

To learn about elasticity try this comparison. Cut one large rubber band to make one long strand of rubber. Then cut a 12-inch (30 cm) strip of plastic from a shopping bag. Now hold both ends of the cut rubber band, and pull. Stretch it as far as it will go. Have someone help you measure the length. Now do the same with the strip from the plastic bag. Which sample stretched the farthest? What happened to each when you let go after stretching?

(Turn to page 29 for the answers)

its original state. When a solid can be stretched and returned to its original shape, it has **elasticity**.

Solids with no elasticity are **brittle**. Ceramic is a brittle solid. If you drop a ceramic cup on the floor, it will not bounce back or stretch. The bonds holding the molecules simply break. The cup shatters.

Solids can also be malleable. Malleable solids can be stretched and pounded into new shapes. Aluminum is a malleable solid. It can be rolled into thin sheets. It can also be molded into objects such as soda cans and silverware.

The most **malleable** metal is gold. It can be pounded and rolled into a sheet so thin that it can be torn with a puff of your breath. Thin sheets of gold are called leaf. It is mostly used for making foods and objects look nice. Gold can also be stretched into thin, hairlike wire. Delicate gold wire is used to make special electronic devices.

Glass is brittle. It will likely break when dropped or stepped on.

There are examples of matter all around you. We use solid matter in countless ways each day. The next time you pick up a pencil or turn on the television, think about the millions of tiny atoms it is made of.

CHAPTER TWO

LOOSE-BONDED LIQUIDS

Ducklings fall in a line behind their mother. Like ducklings,
liquid molecules move freely but stay close together.

In liquid matter, the bonds between molecules are loose and long. The molecules in a liquid stay close to one another, but they move around freely. Young ducklings behave a bit like liquid molecules. Ducklings often swim in a line. Sometimes they swim in a group. Ducklings may separate from each other, but they usually stick close together. They are attracted to one another, but not tied together.

When milk spills, the molecules move and change and a puddle forms.

When water is spilled, it does not scatter into millions of tiny pieces.

It oozes over a surface as one puddle. The molecules move and change

position. But they are still attracted to one another.

Because molecules in a liquid state are not arranged in fixed places, liquid matter flows and has no shape of its own. Liquids take on the shape of their containers. Orange juice, for instance, takes on the shape of the jug. When it is poured, orange juice takes on the shape of the glass. If it is spilled, it spreads out into a thin, irregular puddle.

REAL WORLD SCIENCE CHALLENGE

Water and alcohol have different molecular structures. To discover their differences try this mixing activity. You will need a 2 cup (0.5 L) measuring cup, 1 cup (0.25 L) of water, and 1 cup (0.25 L) of rubbing alcohol. First pour the water into the measuring cup. Record the level of the water. You should observe that the water is at the 1 cup (0.25 L) mark on the measuring cup. What do you think will happen when you add the alcohol to the water?

(Turn to page 29 for the answers)

Lakes, rivers, and oceans are all large bodies of liquid matter. They too take on the shape of their solid matter containers. A lake is the shape of the land basin that holds it. Dirt banks shape the bends of a river. The continents that border oceans also shape them.

Most liquids look about the same when they are in a container. But you can see great differences between liquids when you pour them out. Some liquids are thick and flow slowly. Other liquids are thin and flow quickly. **Viscosity** is a measure of how fast or slow a liquid flows. Water has a low viscosity level. It flows easily. Honey has a high viscosity level. It flows very slowly.

REAL WORLD SCIENCE CHALLENGE

Find a thick, or highly viscous, liquid in your kitchen. Pancake syrup or honey would work well. Pour ¼ cup (60 ml) of liquid into a glass measuring cup. Using a stopwatch, record the time it takes to pour the liquid into a small glass. Repeat the first step. Pour ¼ cup (60 ml) of the liquid into a glass measuring cup. Now ask an adult to help you heat the liquid in a microwave oven for ten seconds. Then pour the liquid into a small glass. Use the stopwatch to record the amount of time it took for the heated liquid to pour. Put the glass in the microwave for ten more seconds. What happens to the viscosity of the liquid when it is reheated?

(Turn to page 29 for the answers)

Temperature can affect viscosity. Thick liquids that are cooled tend to flow more slowly. When a thick liquid is heated, it flows faster.

Most liquids change state depending on temperature. They have a freezing point at which they turn solid. When the temperature of water drops below 32°F (0°C), water begins to freeze. It turns into ice. Ice is water

A snowy winter scene shows what happens to moisture in the air when temperatures fall below a certain point.

in a solid state. Snow and hail are other forms of water in a solid state. If

the temperature is raised above the freezing point, water will change states

again. The ice will melt and return to its liquid form.

Liquid matter also has a boiling point at which it changes to its gas

state. At sea level, water boils at 212°F (100°C). Heating water causes the

molecules to move faster and bounce against each other. As the water gets hotter, the molecules bounce against each other with more and more force. At the boiling point, the molecules break free from the other liquid water molecules. They form gas bubbles that float to the water's surface and pop. They break away from one another and rise into the air. Water in its gas state is called steam.

Liquid matter is vital to life on earth. Our bodies are mostly liquid. We drink water and wash with water. Cars and trucks also depend on liquids. Gasoline and oil help engines run fast and smooth. We depend on liquid to help us through each day.

CHAPTER THREE

MOVING MOLECULES

Iodine crystals change into gas when the molecules are heated.

Matter in the gas state is everywhere. When you move your arms, your hands pass through gases. When you run across the playground, your body races through gases. With each breath you take, you inhale a mixture of gases. Oxygen and nitrogen are two gases that fill your lungs when you breathe.

With matter in the gas state, molecules are far apart. There is much more space between gas molecules than between the molecules in solids and liquids. Gas molecules are always moving. They move in all directions. When gas is not trapped in a container, gas molecules just float away. Then they spread out in the air.

When gas is trapped in a container, it tries to expand as far as it can. Gas molecules expand evenly until they hit the container walls. The **volume**, or space inside the container, is always filled with gas. Even if some gas is released, the gas left behind will stretch out to fill up the empty

21st Century Content

Most people use the word *gas* to identify the fuel that is put into a car or lawnmower. *Gas* is actually a short form of the word *gasoline*. Gasoline is a liquid fuel mixture created by combining forms of natural gas and refined petroleum. In science, the word *gas* is never used to describe gasoline. In science, *gas* describes matter in a gas state.

Gas will expand to fill a container after some of the gas is released.

space. Gas can fill any container. It can fill a small, large, tall, or wide

container. It can fill a container with round sides or jagged sides.

The size of a container affects the gas inside. You could fill a small

container and a large container with the same amount of gas. Inside the

large container the molecules have more space to move. They do not push

against the sides of the container with force. In a small container the gas molecules don't have much room to move around. They push against each other and against the walls of the container with greater pressure. If some of the gas is released, the rest of the gas expands into the container space. The container is still filled with gas, but the gas molecules are no longer being squeezed. The pressure drops.

REAL WORLD SCIENCE CHALLENGE

How does heat affect air pressure? To find out, fill a balloon with air. Use a tape measure or piece of yarn to measure around the balloon. Then place the balloon in the freezer for fifteen minutes. Take it out and measure it again. Did the size of the balloon change? Next place the balloon in the warm sun. What did you observe? Can you explain what is happening to the molecules inside of the balloon as the temperature changes?

(Turn to page 29 for the answers)

In the gas state, temperature is closely related to pressure. When a gas is heated, the molecules move much faster. They bounce against each other with

Natural gas is piped into homes for heating and cooking.

greater speed than when they are cool. Adding heat to gas in a container causes

the pressure to increase.

Pressurized gas can be very useful. When you squeeze the nozzle of

a spray can, gas shoots out very quickly. The force of the spray carries

chemicals where we want them to go. Cooking oil, cleaning fluids, and

paint are some things we find in pressurized spray cans.

One type of gas that many people use every day is called **natural gas**. Natural gas is colorless and odorless. It exists underground. Workers drill deep holes in the ground to collect natural gas. Pipes are placed in the ground to collect the gas. After it is collected, natural gas must be cleaned. Sand, water, and other gases must be removed before it can be used. Natural gas is pumped into many homes where it is used to fuel furnaces, stoves, and water heaters.

Although we can't see most gases, they surround us. Gases fill our lungs, the tires on our cars, and the fuel tanks outside of some homes. Many people depend on gases to heat homes and cook food. Gases can even help us have fun. Gases fill our soccer balls, tennis balls, and basketballs. Our world would be a very different place without gases.

CHAPTER FOUR

MATTER THAT BREAKS THE RULES

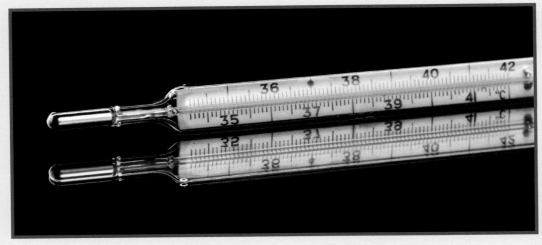

Silver-colored mercury, shown in the tip of a thermometer,
is the only metal that is liquid at room temperature.

We know from experience and scientific experiments what to expect

from most matter. When you see a rock, you know it will feel solid.

When you pour a glass of water, you know what it will feel like when you

swallow it. When you fill a balloon with helium gas, you know that it will

float. Each state of matter has certain constant properties. But there are

exceptions. Some substances don't follow the rules.

Most metals are solid at room temperature. But mercury is an unusual metal. It is the only metal that is a liquid at room temperature. Mercury expands when heated. It was once used in thermometers. Tiny tubes of glass were filled with mercury. When the tubes were heated, the mercury rose. When the mercury stopped moving, a person could read the temperature.

While mercury can help us read temperatures, carbon dioxide can help us keep temperatures low. The solid form of carbon dioxide gas is called dry ice. Dry ice is most often used to keep foods cold. It is much colder than frozen water. And it melts in a very unusual way.

Is the human body solid, liquid, or gas? The answer: a little of all three. The human body is 70 percent liquid. Most of that is water. Our bodies also contain gases. These include oxygen, hydrogen, and nitrogen. But the human body has also solid parts. These include carbon and calcium.

Unlike water, at standard air pressure carbon dioxide does not move through three states of matter. Solid carbon dioxide turns directly into gas. It skips the liquid state. When dry ice is heated above room temperature it appears to give off smoke. The smoke you see is actually carbon dioxide turning into a gas. The dry ice is melting. But it doesn't leave a watery mess. The vapors mix with the air and drift away.

REAL WORLD SCIENCE CHALLENGE

We know that matter can change. But can it be created? Can it be destroyed? To find out, place a piece of fruit in a glass bowl. Tightly cover the bowl with plastic. Let it rest on your kitchen counter for a few days. Observe the fruit each day. Write down what changes you see.

(Turn to page 29 for the answers)

When solid carbon dioxide turns to gas it seems to disappear. While you can't see it, the carbon dioxide still exists. It simply moves to a new place.

When dry ice is dropped into water it turns into gas and appears to give off smoke.

In your daily life, it may seem that matter is being created and

destroyed all the time. But it is not. It just exists in a different state. When

you eat cookies, for instance, they disappear. But the matter that made

up the cookies does not disappear. The cookies are turned into energy.

Your body uses the energy and gets rid of the waste. The waste travels on.

It eventually becomes part of the soil. Soil will help a new seed grow. The

plant will one day be eaten as food. The food will be turned into energy

and the cycle will continue. Matter is recycled over and over again.

REAL WORLD SCIENCE CHALLENGE

Mix up this gooey recipe and observe how a liquid can sometimes act like a solid. Measure ¼ cup (60 ml) of cornstarch into a small bowl. Add 5 to 6 teaspoons (25 to 30 ml) of water. Mix in three to four drops of food coloring if desired. Stir until it is fully mixed. How would you classify this mixture? Is it a solid? Or is it a liquid?

(Turn to page 29 for the answers)

Matter surrounds us. It appears in different states. Each state of matter can

be useful in different ways. Solids, liquids, and gases are all necessary for life to

exist. The next time you look at a piece of matter, think about where it came

from. Think about how it may change and where it will go next.

Real World Science Challenge Answers

Chapter One

Page 8

The rubber band stretched the most. After stretching, the rubber band returned to its original state. The strip of plastic remained stretched. The bonds that connect rubber molecules are coiled like springs. This allows them to bounce back to their starting point. The bonds that hold the molecules in the plastic bag can stretch, but they do not bounce back.

Chapter Two

Page 13

The mixture should measure close to one cup. Alcohol molecules are smaller than water molecules. This allows the alcohol molecules to squeeze between the water molecules. The result is a little bit less than two cups.

Page 15

Heat causes molecules to bounce around. When molecules bounce around they move farther apart. Liquids become less viscous. When cooled, the molecules slow down. The liquid becomes more viscous.

Chapter Three

Page 21

Measurements will vary. The balloon will shrink in size in the freezer. The gas molecules inside the balloon slow down in cool temperatures. When molecules slow down, the pressure falls. The balloon will relax and shrink. The balloon will grow in size when placed in the warm sun. The gas molecules inside the balloon move faster in warm temperatures. When the molecules speed up, the pressure inside the balloon grows. The balloon expands.

Chapter Four

Page 26

Matter cannot be created or destroyed. But it can change from one state to another. As the fruit decays, it will shrink and change shape. You will also see tiny drops of water on the glass. These drops are from gases released from the fruit. The gases condense to a liquid state when they hit the glass.

Page 28

The goop will run like a liquid when you pour it from the bowl. It will feel like a solid when you poke it with your finger. Cornstarch molecules are large and move slowly. When you press or push them, the molecules tangle and stick to one another. When left alone, the molecules flow naturally and the mixture appears as a liquid.

GLOSSARY

atoms (AT ums) smallest particles of matter that have all the chemical properties of the matter

brittle (BRIT tul) easily snapped or broken

chemical bonds (KEM I kull BONDs) forces that join and hold atoms to other atoms to form molecules

elasticity (ee lass TISS ih tee) the ability of a solid to return to its original shape after being stretched or squeezed

malleable (MAL ee uh bull) easily bent or pounded into new shapes

matter (MAT tur) anything that takes up space and has mass. Matter exists mostly as a solid, liquid, or gas

molecules (MOLL uh kyools) two or more atoms joined by chemical bonds

natural gas (NATCH uh rul GAS) underground gas, mostly methane, formed by decaying plant and animal matter trapped between rock layers for millions of years

pressure (PRESH uhr) force pressing on a unit of area or a surface

viscosity (viss KOSS uh tee) a measure of how fast or slowly a liquid flows

volume (VOLL yoom) the amount of space that matter occupies

FOR MORE INFORMATION

Books

Spilsbury, Richard, and Louise A. Spilsbury. *What Are Solids, Liquids, and Gases? Exploring Science with Hands-On Activities.* (In Touch with Basic Science.) Berkeley Heights, NJ: Enslow Elementary, 2008.

West, Krista. *States of Matter: Gases, Liquids, and Solids.* (Essential Chemistry.) New York: Chelsea House, 2008.

Williams, Zella. *Experiments with Solids, Liquids, and Gases.* (Do-It-Yourself Science.) New York: PowerKids, Rosen, 2007.

Web Sites

Chem 4 Kids
www.chem4kids.com/files/matter_intro.html
An online tour of the states of matter, with clear, colorful diagrams

NaturalGas.org
www.naturalgas.org/overview/background.asp
Information about how natural gas is formed and used as an energy source

States of Matter
www.harcourtschool.com/activity/states_of_matter
A fun, interactive way to understand the motion of molecules

States of Matter, Purdue University Department of Chemistry
www.chem.purdue.edu/gchelp/atoms/states.html
Easy-to-understand explanations of the behavior of solids, liquids, and gases

INDEX

ABOUT THE AUTHOR

Heather Miller is the author of more than 35 books for children. She lives in northeast Indiana, where she spends her time reading, writing, and teaching art to young artists. As a young girl she was fascinated by the wonders of science. She continues to be amazed by new scientific discoveries.